BEHIND THE WHEEL:
Poems About Driving

BY JANET WONG

www.poetrysuitcase.com

To my father

PoetrySuitcase.com
4580 Province Line Road
Princeton, NJ 08540
info@PoetrySuitcase.com

These poems were originally published by Margaret K.
McElderry Books, an imprint of Macmillan Children's
Publishing.

Library of Congress Cataloging-in-Publication Data
is available.

ISBN-13: 978-1469909356
ISBN-10: 1469909359

POETRY BOOKS BY JANET WONG

Good Luck Gold

A Suitcase of Seaweed

The Rainbow Hand:
Poems about Mothers and Children

Night Garden:
Poems from the World of Dreams

Knock on Wood:
Poems about Superstitions

TWIST: Yoga Poems

Once Upon A Tiger:
New Beginnings for Endangered Animals

Declaration of Interdependence:
Poems for an Election Year

The *PoetryTagTime* Anthologies
PoetryTagTime
P*TAG
Gift Tag: Holiday Poem

TABLE OF CONTENTS

1 / ASK A FRIEND

You don't always need
to go it alone.
Ask a friend
to give you a ride,
to help you out,
to get you home.

When you've found some better times,
you won't forget, you'll pay him back.
Let your friends be good to you.
Go along for the ride,
face in the wind.

2 / BEHIND THE WHEEL

Forget kindergarten,
sharing.

Everything you need to know

you learn right here
behind the wheel.

Watch out for the other guy.
Keep your eye on your rear.
Thank the old lady who lets you in.
Don't steal someone else's spot.
When you rush to park and
end up hopeless, crooked —

just start over.

3 / CRASH

apologies to David McCord

1.

Crackety-crack
crackety-crack
Grandmother's knuckles
begin their attack
crackety-crack
crackety-crack
crackety-crackety
     crashity
crack.

Before we crash
I reach over
and place my right arm
against Grandmother's chest

the very moment

she reaches over
to me.

2.

After the war with the Japanese
the money markets crashed
and Grandmother's Chinese paper dollars
were worth nothing —

so many missed meals,
never a new dress,
no meat for her baby,
for what—
so she could save those paper dollars
now worth nothing?

And she burned the bills
one by one in the fire,
cooking a pot of rice.

4 / DADDY AND SHIN

I love it when you tell the story,
Daddy —

you and Shin,

> *me and Shin,*
> *we're fresh out of high school*
> *and we're bored*
> *and we're hot*
> *and we are not going to waste*
>
> *our time sitting around*
>
> *so we hop in Shin's car,*
> *drive north up the coast,*
> *wonder*
> *just how far we'll go*
> *on twenty bucks*
> *and still get back*
> *to work the midnight shift.*

I love the part where you roll

> *roll down the hills in neutral,*
> *roll to save some gas*

how could you drive? —
strip the gears? —
how could you drive like that?

When we make it
up to Monterey
we dig for clams
with driftwood sticks,
eat five cans of cold baked beans

and as the tide is coming in
and as the sun is sinking fast,

full of gas
we drive straight

home.

5 / DOWN THE NARROW

Mornings he backed his mother's car out, down the narrow driveway. Sundays he drove the golf cart eighteen holes. Everyone knew he knew how to drive. So why wouldn't he, just two weeks shy of sixteen, drive the Jaguar to deliver his share of their homework? She would be happy to have it that night. She would patch it together, his sentence, hers, her word, his, like a quilt, put together as one.

She would wave to him from her doorway, light in her hair, smile on her face, as he pulled away in that sleek black car.

Mom had gone to the movies with her friend, a woman he had never liked. The friend had left her car keys on the kitchen counter to tease him, to tempt him, he knew. He picked them up. They smelled of perfume. Maybe it was the perfume on his hands that made him think, think as he drove down the hill, what a shame it was for such a fine car to be wasted on her, such a stinking driver —

The sound hit from nowhere like an earthquake, the sound of the hydrant busting loose, ground split open, water gushing, a siren around the corner.

6 / GRANDMOTHER'S CAR

The summer I was eleven
Grandfather put me in charge
of Grandmother,
made me take her on the bus
to the art museum
and the fabric store,
Farmer's Market for lunch.
Put me in charge,
eleven years old,
bus change jingling in my pocket
like a full set of keys.

Here she was, worked her whole life
on the farm and in the restaurant
and all she had
was a five-gallon water bottle
filled with pennies and
nickels and dimes,
a couple of old silver
dollars mixed in.
One night, after her bath,
she sits me down,
says, *I am going to buy you a car.*
Buy you a car, tears in her eyes.
And long as she lives,
I know she is filling her jar,
every penny, every nickel,
every dollar, every dime
dropped in the five-gallon bottle
of bus money
so I can go places
on my own.

7 / HARD ON THE GAS

My grandfather taught himself to drive
rough, the way he learned to live,

push the pedal, hard on the gas,
rush up to 50,
coast a bit,

rush, rest, rush, rest —

When you clutch the bar above
your right shoulder
he shoots you a look that asks,
Who said the ride would be smooth?

8 / HITCHHIKER

A father should be a responsible man.
Should know better.
Set the example for his daughter.

Mine

drives me to school,
swerves over to the side of the road
when we see a hitchhiker
with an algebra book in his hand,
some grimy boy I don't even know.
The boy runs to the car, pants like a dog.
My dad treats him like an old friend,
talks to him about our teams,

listens to him, even,

says to please look out for me.
He says he'll keep an eye on me.
I look into his pimple face
as cold and hard as I can look,

looking not at all
like my father's daughter.

9 / HITCHHIKER 2

Where's a sucker like my dad
when I'm the one who needs a ride?

Anne and I are hitchhiking,
first time for either one.
We took the bus as far as it would go.
Standing by the fields, thumbs out,
we sing to the corn,
have a great time,
a fine time,

too long a time.

A man waves sorry.
His wife gives us the evil eye.
Another man slows to look —
Anne is standing out in front
and Anne is very, very cute
and tall.
I stand behind her,
timid, small.
Can't help but wince
at his creepy face.
He looks at me and speeds away.

That's that.
That's it, two cars with space,
and after half an hour more
we start out walking
all uphill,

and up the hill
with every step
I thank the world
for Dad.

10 / INSURANCE

You need insurance.
You need insurance.
You need insurance.

Can I say it enough?

You're careful.
You're careful.
I know you're careful.
I don't care
how careful you are.
It's those other crazy cars.
What do you do when
a Porsche cuts in front
and you slam on the brakes
(which were never that good),
buckle his back,
buckle your hood,
and the guy gets out
in a fancy suit
and he's fuming mad
and you're madder yet—
The nerve of the jerk!
You're ready to fight
and he whips out his card.

A lawyer.

Oh no.
And the veins in his neck
are starting to show—

You need insurance.
You need insurance.
You need insurance.

Got it?

11 / INSURANCE FOR TEENAGE DRIVERS: A NEW PLAN

First incident:

Offender must stand
in the middle
of a busy intersection
for one whole day,
directing traffic.

Second incident:

Direct traffic,
head shaved bald.

Third incident:

Direct traffic,
head shaved bald,
singing in a microphone,
flanked by parents
dressed in pajamas.

12 / JUMP-START

can't turn over
battery's dead

need
jumper cables
in
my
head

clamp them on
start me up

pour some coffee
in my cup
dark strong coffee

start me up

13 / KNUCKLES

Used to be she would
grab the bar
above her shoulder.
I'd start the car,
she'd grab the bar.
Sometimes she'd put
both hands up,
her left arm shielding
her face.

Now that I have been driving
one full year
she has stopped doing that.
Sits, hands in lap,
cracking knuckles,
first pushing down
on fingers bent at right angles
to crack the big joints,
then pushing straightened fingers
side to side to crack the middle joints,
then pressing each folded finger
into itself
to crack the top joints.
She cracks them all
as many times as they will give,
moves next to the neck
and a shrug of her shoulders
to crack the back.

I knew a girl named Liz, from Texas,

who showed us once at lunchtime
how she could crack her hips,

swivel, crack, crack

and we all started swiveling
and cracking up,
our heads spinning dizzy.

14 / LESSONS IN BRAKING

Three years old:

Each time your mother brakes
on the curve down the hill
where your swimming lessons are,
your juice streaks your cheek,
flies in the front seat.
You wash your sticky face
blowing bubbles in the pool.

Brake *before* you make a turn.

Nine years old:

Your mother curses at the cars
cutting right in front of her
in this crowded exit lane.
She doesn't want to hit them, so
she keeps your car a good way back,
and when she feels the space is fine,
then another car slips in.

You don't need *too much* braking space.

Fifteen years old:

You're singing to the radio
in your mother's brand-new car
with four-wheel drive and ABS.*

Your mother's sitting in the back,
trying not to watch you drive.
You hit a patch of ice. You slide.
Pump the brakes! your mother screams.
You pump the brakes and spin right out.

With ABS, steady braking is the best.

*ABS: antilock braking system

15 / LIKES OF US

We go to the auto show
knowing we can afford
nothing
except maybe a hot dog
or a bag of popcorn.
Still, we go,
picking up the brochures,
trying the doors
of the new Mercedes
with our buttery fingers.
The new Mercedes.
Locked.
Lexus.
Locked.
Audi.
Locked.
Infiniti.
Locked, all locked
to the likes of us.
We walk and walk around some more
until our bags grow heavy
and our feet feel sore,
then pile into the Chevy van,
take our shoes off,
wiggle our toes.
We settle back.
We watch the people.
We watch the people waiting in line,
waiting in line to fill out forms —
sick to see them hope so much

to win this van —
but who's to say how luck will land?
We slip our shoes back on again,

get in line.

16 / NEED TO READ

need to read
to pass the test

scratch
those signs into my brain

merge
yield
steep grade

read the handbook
read it again
read it again

sleep on it

dream those signs
dream

the license *is* mine

17 / NEIGHBORS

In Grandmother's village
you didn't go
where you couldn't walk.
You knew everyone,
their dirty laundry,
their loud songs.

On our street
we know so little, it seems,
about the good quiet neighbors we see
once a week at the market
a mile away.
Rack of lamb?
Looks like a storm's coming in, huh.
They head to the cheese.
We steer the opposite way, to fruit,
and when we end up at the checkout
at the same time,
we park our carts
in different lines.

Then it's out to the cars.
Trunks are loaded up.
I turn the key right away,
lay our claim to back out first.
They follow us home
down our hill.
Their headlights
throw shadows,
our big empty heads
bobbing on the dash.

18 / OK

You hate to hear this preachy stuff
again and again.
OK OK OK —
I'll say it once, then.
Don't drink and drive.

Sure.

Who doesn't like a little fun
and when you go to a party
and you drink a drink or two
the whole world dances,
dances with you,

the whole world —
yeah.
Except the girl
who died last night,
bled to death
in the family car
sideswiped
by a party drunk.

Next time you start on drink number two
think about that girl, OK?
See her long hair swinging,
her thin legs dancing,
laughing, laughing, just like you
once upon a time.

19 / ONE HAND ON THE WHEEL

You know the kind.
Your father shouts at them.
Your mother's one of them.
White knuckles
clutch the wheel,
hands at 11 o'clock and 1 o'clock,
30 in a 50 zone,
stops for invisible cars.

Can't go far.

My mother *was* one of them
when —
who knows what happened.

Now she's driving 65,
one hand holding a cup of coffee,
one hand on the wheel

and we have no idea
where we're headed.

Maybe the problem with Dad is not a problem with Dad. $800 on an old truck, $200 to paint it and another $1500 to bring it home after it catches on fire going 50 might be crazy to some, but maybe a curse is to blame, and we should have seen it coming in the first place in the plates, 1LMN (as in lemon) 444 (as in the old Chineseleaving a sour taste in your mouth every morning as you puzzle over what new thing is wrong. Maybe LMN does not stand for lemon, but means *Like More Nonsense?*, a question the truck seems to ask as it breaks down in an even more ridiculous way every other day. Maybe LMN means some strange thing in Hungarian or Danish or Czech; LMN: (noun) he who is destined to pull to the side of the road.

Poor Dad: What if his plate had read 1LKY001 instead?

21 / OOXXOXO

Everyone could see it
in the driveway
with an almost shiny wax job
except in the rusted spots
and a big red bow
stretched bumper to bumper,
hooked in the dent at the back:

HPYBRTD
CUTIEPI
SUPRGRL
YRTRFC
YRTRIFC
OOXXOXO (HGSNKSS)
NX TIM NU
(next time a new one for you) —
PROMISE.

22 / PLAIN AND SIMPLE

I like the look of a Land Rover,
old Avanti, Citroën.
Who says you can't dream?
Who would know from the looks of me
in my rusting Civic, bland,
nothing much to shout about —

tell me, would you know who I am?

You don't have to pamper me.
Don't have to worry
someone will steal me away.
Plain and simple, you can count on me
never to give you trouble.

Count on me.

23 / PRISONER

The baby
is crying his head off
and you feel so helpless,
so torn—

Libbie said they gave her
a $500 ticket when she took Ella
out of the car seat,
Ella so sick and all
and still the cop cut her no slack—

but the baby is back there hollering
trying to make you
take him out
of the car seat
and you don't know
and you don't know
and you don't know what to do—

How many times
have you rolled your eyes
when you hear them say,
It hurts me more than you?

24 / REST STOP

We've been driving all day long.
Look how far we have gone,
and in the pouring rain, no less,
through wind that almost
blew us off the road.
We're on our way.
You say it's *only* four more hours,
Can't you make it?
Can't you last?

But oh, my back, my aching back,
my back is sore.
My eyes are weak.
My feet feel thick
with too much blood.

I need to stop. Rest. Sleep.
Come, won't you dream with me?

25 / RESTRAINT
for my friends at Polytechnic

When the poet came
to visit our school
to make us write some poetry,
people from our families
turned into trees
and owls and slugs.
My sister was a hurricane.

End of class,
Jim raised his hand.

My parents are like seat belts.
They're always around me —
But I guess
they help keep me safe.

The room was quiet.
Then a hum spread all around.
I wished I could have thought like Jim.

Things are different at my home.
Sometimes you wonder if they care.
But when you mess up — WOOOMPH! —
they're there, like air bags,
in your face.

26 / SEND ME A SIGNAL

send me a signal
you need help
on the road

light up a flare

where the sparks
will fly
sting
my blind eyes

let me show
let me show
let me show

how
i care

27 / SHORT SIGHTED

They've never had someone so short
in driver's ed,
so they didn't know what to do
when my foot didn't touch
the pedals.
Stuck a thin block
on the gas,
a thick block
on the brake
so my legs could reach.

If only they could stretch me enough
so I can see
where I'm going—

28 / SLOW ON THE CURVE

Mr. M says the test men make the girls
parallel park first thing, to fluster us so we'll
break down, quit at the start. My brother
says the women flirt with the boys and it's
so easy, all right turn, right turn, as long as
you smile back. They never test The Curve,
the freeway ramp five stories high, floating
at an angle to dump you in the sky. Mr. M
laughs when I slow to a crawl as The Curve
pops up beyond the hood, says we're safe,
centrifugal force on our side. Everyone else
is quiet. It's not for nothing that I am getting
a solid C in driver's ed.

I hear seat belts click shut as we head into
the bend.

29 / SPEED LIMIT

Some places
you go 37 in a 35 zone
and you're nailed.
You should have known.

Some places you go 70
and still they pass you in the fast lane,
Volvos, even —

But just when you start to feel slow,
you see the red, white and blue
in the corner of your eye
and ease on the gas
as the cop speeds by —

The others hit their brakes real hard,
blushing red.
The cop's not blind.
No, but he has set his mind
to get *one* car,
and can you believe
there's good in the world,
and he's got the guy
who shook his fist
and growled at you —

You set the cruise at 65
as you take the lead.

30 / STUFF

You can stuff the glove compartment
the way your mother stuffs you
on Thanksgiving,
so nothing fits,
Come on, just one little itty bit more —

or you can keep it lean,
bare bones,
registration, insurance, flashlight, book —

oh, but why not
one picture of your parents
taped to the back
of their birthday card to you,
so they can feel safe
that when you are lost

at least you will not forget
where you call home.

31 / THREE-WAY STOP

The old lady got there first,
and you got there second,
but here he comes, that jerk in his truck,
trying to push his way through—
So you charge to block him off,
you charge, by golly,
to stick up for what is right—

and you crash,
ding his tail,
smash your light.

32 / TOGETHER

The problem with you, B,
was a car problem,

was there never was
anywhere to sit and talk
without feeling like animals
in the zoo, nervous, watched.

Forget about anything else
when weeks on weeks

you can't even find
a good place
to joke around,
to laugh loud.

When we ran into each other
red in the face

at the library
or in the computer room
and stood near the door
didn't you — I swear I could —

I swear I could hear our own whispers
bounce off the walls,

keyboards gone quiet,
pages unturned,
my own breath short.
I never could hear you breathe.

So those words I saved for you, B,
stayed quiet, hiding,

multiplying inside of me,
growing into paragraphs
and whole dissertations,
screenplays,

a heavy bookcase I dragged around
day and night.
When Z came along offering a ride
I was tired, so tired

I needed a lift.
I did not plan
to abandon you,
to leave you behind,

but sitting alone in the car with him,
speaking my mind

for ten minutes
the whole way home
and almost an hour outside my house,
those words I scripted for you

flew out of my mouth, so full and hot
they fogged the windows up

as we talked about big things,
children, college,
dreams,

you, even.

Nothing else happened, just talk,
but right then
I fell in love with him and
fell out of love with you,

his voice
and my voice
and the motor running
together.

33 / WAIT TILL WHEN

How many times
did you fall in love
this week
and find yourself
stuck
as usual,

no place to go
but
school and home again,
home to pine away—

where there's nothing fun
to do—

so no wonder
that sliver of a smile
you thought you saw
keeps growing huge.
Wait
till
when

you're free
to drive,
not see the same old same old
every day—

Oh, what wonderful trouble
then.

34 / WHEN A COP STOPS YOU

When a cop stops you,
what can you do?

Grab your leg and moan in pain?

I would if I could,
but I know I would laugh.
So I sit there, waiting,
shrinking fast,
humble, quiet.
Stupid. Sweet.

When the cop walks up,
I stare at his feet.
I give him my papers.
I listen. I nod.
When he lets me go—

Thank God.

35 / YOU HAVE GOT TO

I don't go to church.
I can't say for sure
I believe in much.
But you've got to believe,
when you drive like crazy,
spin in the rain
in front of a bus and
straighten out
no harm done,

you've got to believe

there's a place for you
in this amazing world—

and you owe it to yourself,
you have got to
keep on going until
you arrive.

AUTHOR'S NOTE

When I was a freshman at UCLA, I volunteered for the Prison Coalition, tutoring teen boys in a juvenile detention center. The most-requested book was the driver's handbook. I was sure that their first days out, those boys would march down to the DMV to take their driving tests. My primary inspiration for this book was my memory of so many afternoons of reading about driving.

The second reason I wrote this book is that I'd just finished writing *The Rainbow Hand: Poems about Mothers and Children* and I wanted now to write a book honoring my father. Some of our most special times took place when he was teaching me to drive. Wanting to keep me relaxed, he would chat away, telling me stories while I drove around our neighborhood. My favorite story was about him and his buddy Shin, and the day they drove from Los Angeles to Monterey with hardly any money, shifting into neutral and rolling down hills to save gas. On the subject of gas (a different sort): they didn't have money for food, so when they got to Monterey, they ate what they'd hastily grabbed from a cupboard at Shin's house before leaving that morning: five cans of baked beans. Of course they farted all the way home!

My first car was my mother's hand-me-down old Toyota Corolla, made fresh with a coat of bright paint to supposedly match my favorite nail polish. My favorite nail polish was actually a coppery rust color but the auto body shop had painted the car fire-engine red. It wasn't exactly what I'd expected — but its show-stopping (or cop-stopping) color was only one of its many "charms." The most-charming thing was the way the non-powered steering wheel shook violently at 55mph, as if we were driving through miles of earthquakes. Still, it was a set of wheels, it was my freedom, and it was a symbol of my parents' trust and love.

ABOUT THE AUTHOR

Janet Wong is the author of more than two dozen books for children and teens. She has been honored with the Claremont Stone Center Recognition of Merit, the IRA Celebrate Literacy Award, and her appointment to two terms on the NCTE Commission on Literature and also two terms on the Excellence in Children's Poetry Award Committee. A frequent speaker at schools and conferences all over the world, Janet Wong has performed at the White House and her work has been featured on CNN, Fine Living's Radical Sabbatical, and The Oprah Winfrey Show.

www.janetwong.com

IF YOU LIKED THIS BOOK . . .
LOOK FOR GOOD LUCK GOLD

Fresh, honest, and not at all reverential, these poems are simple dramatic monologues about growing up Asian American. The lines are short and very easy to read; the voices are strongly personal. The ethnicity is strongly individualized, but whether the subject is food, family, or immigration, Wong moves beyond stereotype. This Asian isn't quiet and good at math ("Me. I like to shout"). The pain of being an outsider and the sting of bigotry are both individual and universal . . . In a scene in a railroad cafe, where no one will serve a Chinese child and her father, she pulls him by the hand to get out of there. "We're not equal. We're better," she says. — *Booklist*

Reading this when I was growing up would have felt like discovering a new best friend. Reading it now as an adult brought a flood of insights to familiar situations. Janet Wong has written poetry in the best sense of the word — not just Asian American adolescent poetry, but simply a fine book of poetry for readers of all ages and backgrounds. — *International Examiner*

Through a good range of subject matter, Wong's rich Asian heritage is revealed along with a profound love and appreciation of family and friends. — *Mid-South Children's Book Review*

Made in the USA
Lexington, KY
21 June 2014